ISBN 978-1-334-47258-9
PIBN 10675952

1 MONTH OF
FREE
READING

at
www.ForgottenBooks.com

By purchasing this book you are
eligible for one month membership to
ForgottenBooks.com, giving you
unlimited access to our entire
collection of over 700,000 titles via
our web site and mobile apps.

To claim your free month visit:
www.forgottenbooks.com/free675952

lins (T.) Examination of the Principles of
an improved system of Banking and the
means of carrying it into effect   Lond. 1831

'tain Regenerated: or, the National Debt
shew capable of immediate redemption.
                                    Bridgnorth, 1831

nittivell's (Rev. R.) Letter to Lord Althorp, &c. &c. &c.
on Mr. Attwood's motion for enquiry touching
the state of the Currency, the cause and
key-stone of the late awful disturbances
throughout the Country.   Halesworth, 1831

'n versus Currency; or the Forgotten Addresses
presented to Parliament at the close of the
_ session.   Lond. 1831

allatin's (A.) Considerations on the Currency and
Banking system of the United States.
                                    Philadelphia, 1831

'derations to all classes on the Necessity and
Equity of a National Banking and Annuity
system, &c.   Lond. 1831

'itorical sketch of the Bank of England: with
an examination of the Question as to the
prolongation of the exclusive privileges of

PRINTED BY JAMES COLSTON,
EAST ROSE STREET, HANOVER STREET,
EDINBURGH.

A

LETTER

TO

Mr. ATTWOOD,

ON THE CURRENCY QUESTION;

BY CAPTAIN FORMAN, R. N.

Author of "Letters on the Real Cause of our Commercial Distress" Price 1s.

and "A Letter to Mr. Cobbett, on the Currency," Price 1s.

Price Sixpence.

LONDON:

LONGMAN, REES, ORME, BROWN, AND GREEN,

AND WASON AND FOXWELL,

SHEPTON-MALLET.

MDCCCXXXI.

PRINTED BY
WASON AND FOXWELL,
SHEPTON-MALLET.

A LETTER,

&c.

PILTON, NEAR SHEPTON-MALLET, JANUARY 17th. 1831.

Sir

I do not write this in the hope of inducing you to become a convert to my opinions ; but as you refer me to certain productions, which you say contain much, "both as to facts and arguments," which is at present unknown to me, I must either submit to an imputation which I do not deserve, or make some reply to the above insinuation.

You say that you do not concur in many of my opinions, and refer me, for further information, to Hansard's Parliamentary Debates, and Sir James Graham's pamphlet on Corn and Currency ; but you do not point out a single paragraph, in my pamphlet, in which either the premises or the conclusions deduced from them, are untenable ; though that, Sir, *if it had been in your power*, might have been done in as few words ; and I must add would have been far more convincing. With respect to Hansard's Debates, I cannot procure a sight of them without purchasing the work ; but I have discussed, and, *I think*, refuted all the arguments in support of your side of the question, that are to be found in the recent speeches, writings, and lectures, upon this subject, of Mesrs. Western, Sadler, and Cobbett, and it is paying but a poor compliment to the understandings of these Gentlemen, to infer, as you do, that in making their appeals to the public they have been so stupid as to omit the only arguments that were worth listening to. I cannot afford to purchase Hansard's Debates, but, on your recommendation, I have just read Sir James Graham's pamphlet. He quotes you frequently, and, from the sample he has given of the arguments that are to be found in Handsard, I will venture to predict that, when you make your *promised* motion, you will introduce no argument, that bears upon this question, but what has already been fully refuted, either directly or indirectly, in one or the other of my *two* pamphlets. If I had met with Sir James Graham's pamphlet before I wrote mine to Mr. Cobbett, I should have made great use of it, for he has furnished me with the very documents I was in search of ; and I am gratified to find that these documents confirm all that it was my object to prove ; while they manifestly contradict the conclusions which he, by a strange process of reasoning, has endeavoured to deduce from them.

The following extracts are from his Tables,

Years.	Amount of Bank of England Notes.	Price of Gold per oz.		
1784	£9,160,470	£4	2s.	0d.
1816	£26,681,398	£3	18s.	6d.
	Bank of England & Country Notes.			
1813	£46,704,445	£5	10s.	0d.
1814	£51,000,832	£5	1s.	8d.
	Bank of England Notes.	Price of Wheat per quarter		
1792	£11,149,809	43s.		
1794	£10,697,924	51s.		
1795	£13,539,163	71s.		
1796	£10,909,694	76s.		
1792	£11,149,809	43s.		
1797	£ 8,601,964	52s.		
1796	£10,909,694	76s.		
1803	£15,967,094	56s.		

These extracts Sir, are taken from Sir James Graham's book; and if common sense had anything to do with the deciding of this question, there could be no hesitation in pronouncing that his opinion, upon this question, which he holds in common with you Sir, and most of the Members of the House of Commons, is contradicted by facts, and therefore cannot possibly be true.

I am willing to admit that *some* facts, which are exhibited in these tables, lean in the direction which your theory requires; but even in these instances that seem to favour your side of the question, the fall of prices does not correspond in degree, with the amount of the contraction, which would have been the case, if it had been solely occasioned by that measure. To sum up in the manner of a judge, one half of the evidence *directly* contradicts the charge; and the other *barely* admits the possibility, but does not pretend to vouch for the fact. This is your case, Sir; and permit me to ask you where you can find a jury that will allow such a charge to be valid?

I shall now Sir, take the liberty of submitting a case to your especial consideration; and though I do not flatter myself with the hope that you will personally favour me with your opinion upon it, you must do it in the House of Commons, or you will forfeit all claim to the character of an impartial and unbiassed advocate of the cause which you have taken in hand. Do not, Sir, follow a bad example; do not, in imitation of Messrs. Sadler and Western, endeavour to shuffle out of a dilemma and avoid a discussion by affecting to despise what you find you are unable to answer; for whatever those Gentlemen may *pretend* to think of my letters upon this subject, if the excellency of a composition consists in good sense and sound argument, and not merely in gaudy flowers and fanciful decorations, these letters, to say the least of them, are far beyond the reach of such intellects as they possess.*

If the rise in the price of provisions, which took place immediately after the commencement of the late war in 1793, had been occasioned solely by a depreciation of the currency, in consequence of an extension of its amount, as you contend, the farmer, with the exception of having additional war taxes to pay, would have been precisely in the same condition that he was in before the rise ; and therefore it must be evident, by the continuing improved condition, both of the Land-holders and farmers throughout the country, *as the prices advanced,* that the greatest part of this rise in the price of provisions, if not the whole of it, *as I suspect,* was a real increase, occasioned by an increased demand ; and not a nominal increase, occasioned by a depreciation of the currency.

Suppose A. B. to farm his own Estate, which, of course, would be rent free, and that the annual produce of this Farm, on an average of five years ending in 1792, amounted in value to £200.

Suppose again that the annual produce of the same Farm, without any alteration or improvement in the culture of it, on an average of five years ending in 1810. amounted to £400 ; and that the aforesaid A. B. during both these periods, expended the whole of his income, but never went beyond it. In this case, the nominal increase of his income must have amounted to £200 ; and in order to ascertain how

---

* As to Mr Cobbett, he is beneath contempt. He suffered some very severe animadversions of mine, on his Lectures on the Currency, to pass without comment, either in his Political Register, or in his subsequent Lectures on the same subject ; though, out of regard to his character, if he had not known himself to be in the wrong, he would, undoubtedly, have made an attempt to defend his doctrines against my aspersions. Some time after the publication of that pamphlet, he announced his intention of giving a course of those lectures at Bath ; but on my giving him public warning, that, as soon as they should be reported in one of the Bath papers, I would publish my remarks upon them by the same vehicle, he took care to slink out of the discussion. Without offering any excuse for this breach of promise : though he must have known that the curiosity excited by my public challenge, would have crammed the theatre every night ; and he would certainly have filled his pockets, however he might have been despised by his auditors.

But, whatever might have been his motive for not giving his promised lectures at Bath, he felt, or fancied it necessary to justify his non-acceptance of my *repeated* challenges, and accordingly in a letter to the Editor of the Bath Journal, under the signature of Candidus Mr. Cobbett himself, or an alter idem, informed the Bath public that my pamphlet was a flimsy production unworthy the notice of such a man as Mr. Cobbett ; and that I was evidently incompetant to discuss this question, as I had never read his Essay on Paper versus Gold. Upon this, I immediately procured a sight of his Essay, and published a letter, directly addressed to him, in which I completely refuted all the arguments that are worth notice in that work of sophistry. A copy of this letter was sent to his Office ; and what was the result? The pamphlet to this day has not been answered! During the whole of this controversy and in every other in which I have been concerned, I cannot accuse myself of having passed over one argument which I believed to have been against me ; and sorry am I to be obliged to say that the same liberal conduct has not been pursued towards me.

much of this increase was merely nominal, and how much of it was a real improvement, we must examine the state of his expenditure at both these periods. Deduct from the sum of £200, the price of all the commodities he was annually enabled to purchase *above* what he could at the former period, together with the increased value of all those goods which he was formerly accustomed to purchase; deduct these two sums from £200, and the remainder, if there should be any, you may, if you please, attribute to the depreciation of the currency; but, if you will make the calculation, you will find it too trifling to deserve consideration.

Again ; The reduction of taxation since the return of peace, has been at *least*, as great in proportion to the whole amount, as the contraction of the currency, and therefore it necessarily follows *(and Sir James Graham admits it)* that the real amount of Taxes would not be greater than they were during the war, even if the intrinsic value of the coin had been raised in the same proportion that it had been contracted.

Now, Sir, *for the sake of argument*, I will admit, *though I know the thing to be impossible*, that the value of the currency has been raised in the manner your hypothesis requires, and I call upon you, as you would be esteemed a man of sense and discernment, I call upon you, Sir, to shew in what manner this measure, supposing that it really took place, could have been productive of such general distress, If the fall of prices, as you maintain had been occasioned solely by an alteration in the value of the currency, the price of all goods, of every description, would have been reduced in the same proportion, the barter, or real price would have been precisely the same, and every individual, with his *nominally* reduced income, might have purchased as muchgoods of every description as he could have done before his income was reduced. If the Landholders, as they must have done, if they had possessed the common principles of honesty and integrity, if the landholders had reduced their rents and the farmers their labourers' wages, in the same proportion as the value of the coin was improved, the condition of all these classes, together with that of the manufacturers and shopkeepers, would have-been, *at least*, * as good as it was before. By your own admission as well as by parliamentary documents, it is evident that the nominal value of the taxes has been reduced in as great proportion as their real value has increased ; and therefore it necessarily follows that every individual, in each of these classes, might have paid his share of the *nominally* reduced taxes, and have purchased the same quantity of goods with his *nominally* diminished income, as he had formerly done with his

---

* If the value of the currency had been raised in the manner you suppose, the property of the fundholders and public annuitants would have been improved. while that of all the other classes would have continued the same; and therefore, in the same proportion as the property of the fundholders had improved, they would have had more money to lay out *for the benefit of the community.*

nominally greater income. If as Sir James Graham asserts, there could have been any landholders so stupidly ignorant, as to mortgage parts of their estates on the supposition that high prices would last for ever, when every plough boy could have told them, that, as the war brought high prices, the peace would inevitably bring back low prices ; if there were any landholders whose estates were incumbered with mortgages and annuities at the time of the change, these landowners, and these alone, *or the farmers who rented of them*, would suffer loss; but even this would not diminish the general stock of the community, because the mortgagee would gain what was lost by the mortgager ; and, to make the most of it, it might occasion a *partial* loss among *some* of the farmers, but could not possibly account for the general distress, which is the object of the present enquiry.

Long before a paper currency was introduced into this country, it was observed that war brought high prices, and peace low prices. Hence originated the proverb "that peace brings plenty ; and as the same cause must necessarily produce the same effect, it is easy to account for the present low prices (as I have shewn in the fifth motto at the head of my letter to Mr. Cobbett) without having recourse to these whimsical speculations, which can only serve to amuse the imaginations of the landed gentlemen, without improving their circumstances ; and must ultimately bring both the proposers and adopters of propositions, which are so manifestly absurd, into general contempt.

I have now, Sir, only to add that, as this letter is meant to be public, you are of course at liberty to shew it to whomsoever you please ; but I particularly request that it may be placed in the hands of Sir James Graham, because I never wish to attack any person's opinions without giving him the opportunity of defending them. I shall read your speech with great attention, though, to be candid, I do not expect to derive much information from it

I am, Sir

Your very obedient Servant
WALTER FORMAN.

---

* If the fact could be ascertained. I have no doubt that it would be found that those estates, which are incumbered with contracts of this nature, that took place *before* the return of peace, bear but a small proportion to the whole of the landed property throughout the kingdom ; for it is impossible to believe that any man, who was in possession of his senses, could have mortager his estate, or have saddled it with annuities, on the supposition that the war prices would be kept up after the return of peace; and indeed it is evident, by numerous debates in both houses of Parliament during the war, that such an idea was never entertained by the landed gentlemen in either house. That there are some *(comparatively)* few estates in the country that are deeply mortgaged I make no doubt, but this can only be attributed to extravagance on the part of the mortager, and not to his ignorance of what was likely to take, place. As far as these mortgages are concerned, I do not see how any remedy can be applied; but, with respect to the annuities, if there are any of this description, the Lord Chancellor, as the law now stands, is, *I believe*, or, at all events, ought to be, empowered to reduce their amount in the same proportion as the rentals have diminished; provided a fair presumption can be produced in support of the supposition, that the testators themselves would have made similar alterations in their bequests, if they had been aware of what was likely to take place.

The following Propositions, upon which a better system of Taxation is grounded, is most respectfully submitted to the consideration of the Members of the House of Commons.

1st. A general Property tax is the fairest and least oppressive of any tax that can possibly be levied on the community, inasmuch as it makes all classes contribute to the wants of the state in exact proportion to the amount of their property ; and those only could be inconvenienced by it, who have hitherto paid *less* than their fair proportion.

2nd. A Property tax is the only tax that can reach absentees ; and therefore it would bring a small accession to the revenue, without increasing the burdens of the people.

3rd. If a property tax were to be substituted for the *whole* of the Excise and Assessed taxes, together with the Custom dues on those articles, the importation of which would not interfere with the profits of our own manufacturers, the public would gain, *probably*, more than a million sterling (after deducting a reasonable remuneration for the past services of those who would be deprived of their offices) by adopting a cheaper and more effectual mode of collecting the revenue.

4th. A tax on the necessaries of life is indirectly, a tax upon labour and is therefore *doubly* injurious to trade ; a tax on property is not, either directly or indirectly, a tax on labour, and consequently a property tax, in lieu of a tax on the necessaries of life, would be beneficial to the community.

5th. A mere reduction of taxation would benefit the fund holders and other annuitants, who have profited much by the fall of prices, in a greater degree than those who have suffered in consequence of it; but a tax on property would make the annuitants, and especially the great monied men, pay more than they do at present, and, so far, would be a relief to the other classes.

6th. If Corn might be imported duty free, the price of bread, taking the average, would be reduced very nearly thirty per cent; and hence it follows that the non-importation act, operates as a tax to that amount on that one article, without adding one penny to the revenue of the community,

7th. A free importation of corn would either add very materially to the comforts of the poor, or else diminish the expense of maintaining them; and, in the latter case, would make a reduction of the poor-rates of, *probably*, more than one million sterling.

8th. The land was made chargeable with the maintenance of the poor, on the understanding, of course, that no corn would be imported from abroad ; and therefore it follows that the poor-rates, though paid at first, by the farmers, are ultimately defrayed by the consumers, who pay so much more for their corn on that account.

9th. It is evident, by the preceding proposition, that if corn were to be imported duty free, the landed interest ought no longer to be burdened with a tax upon land, or, exclusively, with the maintenance of the poor; for, in that case, that class would be more heavily taxed than any other portion of the community.

10th. If corn were to be imported free of duty, the reduction in the price of that article would be equal in amount to the poor-rates and land tax combined, (unless we are to understand that parish paupers are furnished with meat as well as bread,) and therefore a *general* tax on property, to that amount, *with a free importation of corn*, would be no inconvenience to the consumer; while the measure would tend to reduce, or, at all events, keep down the price of labour, and diminish very considerably the expense of maintaining the poor.

11th. Sir James Graham, in his pamphlet, proposes to allow wheat to be imported, at all times, on paying a fixed duty of fifteen shillings per quarter. The object of this measure is evidently to tax the consumer, to the amount of fifteen shillings per quarter, for the payment of the poor-rates and land tax; which might just as well be done by a tax upon property.

12th. The object of my proposal is to reduce the price of bread, and, with it, the price of labour; while what Sir James Graham proposes, by keeping up the price of bread, must necessarily raise, or keep up, the price of labour. The farmers, by Sir James Graham's plan, would have to pay at least two shillings a week more to *each* of their labourers than they would if my plan were to be adopted; and therefore, so far, the farmers, and the manufacturers as well, would be benefitted by giving my plan the preference to that of Sir James Graham: unless we are to suppose that this tax, of fifteen shillings per quarter on wheat, would be more than sufficient to cover the poor-rates and land tax; and then it would be unfair.

13th. Whatever may be thought advisable, with respect to a free importation of corn, it could not possibly be attended with any inconvenience, to the community, to substitute a property, or modified income tax, for the Excise and Assessed taxes, together with *all* the duties on Tea, Coffee, Sugar, and Sea-borne Coals; because, as this is the cheapest mode of collecting the revenue, it would operate as a gain to the public, to the amount of, *probably*, more than one million sterling annually.

14th. It may be set down as an axiom in political economy, that an increase of population helps very materially to enrich a country that is but thinly inhabited; and to impoverish a country, like England, that is over-crowded with inhabitants. Government ought therefore to encourage colonization as much as possible, so far as it can be done consistently with the comfort and happiness of the emigrants; because by so doing, we should benefit the poor labourers themselves, and di-

diminish our own expenses for the maintenance of the poor, at the same time that we enriched the places where they are to be sent.

15th. Most of the unfortunate persons, who have just received sentence of transportation, for the recent commotions, are agricultural labourers ; and would, of course, be very useful, as agricultural labourers, in New South Wales, where the price of labour is very high. If Government therefore would permit their wives and families to go out with them, they would, in all probability, become useful members of society ; and, in a very little time, would amply repay this country the expense of transporting them, by creating an additional demand for our manufactures.*

Some Observations on a Reform of Parliament.

It is not my design in this sketch to give a finished picture of a mode of representation in which all classes of the community would be fairly, as well as virtually, represented; but to direct the attention of Parliament to a very large class of the community that can hardly be said to be even virtually represented ; and show how this class might be represented in Parliament, in such a way as, I am persuaded, would be perfectly satisfactory to themselves, without running any risk of destroying the balance of the Constitution.

The persons who compose this class are chiefly labourers ; and if they had been really represented in Parliament last session, their just grievances would have been listened to, and, in a great measure, redressed, before they were urged on, partly by their distresses, and partly by the artful insinuations of unprincipled mischief-makers, to the commission of crimes, which never would have taken place if they had been under the influence of better advisers. Instead of making inflammatory * harangues and virulent addresses, to the people, in abuse of the ministry, for not doing what, as ministers, it was not in their power to perform, the real advocates of the labouring classes, would have suggested to the gentlemen of landed property the necessity, the absolute necessity of lowering their rents and making their tenants rise the price of wages, as the only means of preventing a conflagration, which was on the point of bursting forth ; and which has since spread itself all over the kingdom. As the representatives of the labourers, they would have been aware of the danger, and, by pointing it out, not to the ministers, but to the land-owners, it might have been avoided.

---

* If the postage of letters were reduced one half, it would be a very great convenience to the poorer classes of the community, who have their affections as well as their betters; and the postage on the additional letters, that would be written in consequence of this measure, would go far towards making up the deficiency of revenue that would otherwise be sustained.

* It is difficult to determine whether the lectures and writings of Mr. Cobbett, or the inflammatory speeches of Mr. Sadler and some others, *out of Parliament*, were most instrumental in producing the late disturbances.

The labourers ought to be really represented, as well as the other classes of the community; but universal suffrage is the only means, which has *yet* been suggested of extending the elective franchise to them; and, as they are more numerous than all the other classes put together, universal suffrage would put the whole power in their hands, and place the constitution at the mercy of the very persons who have already done so much mischief; and who certainly are very ill qualified to take upon themselves the office of legislators. I am aware that universal suffrage has been successfully tried in the United States of North America; and it may be argued that as it works well in that country, we have grounds to believe that it would [answer equally well in England. To this I reply that the state and condition of the two countries are very dissimilar. The United States are, at present, very thinly inhabited ; the prices of labour, in consequence of the great demand for it, are very high ; and, generally speaking, the condition of the labourers is nearly equal to that of their employers. At present, the American labourers could not even hope to gain any thing by a change; but if ever these states should become as densely populated as England is, the price of wages will fall equally low ; one half of the labourers will be thrown out of employ ; and then nothing but a military disposition will save that country from universal anarchy.

In my opinion, if universal suffrage should once be conceded to the people, or rather to the demagogues who wish to influence them, al l the other barriers of the constitution would very soon be broken down; and, as has been the case before, both in France and England * we should have to wade through convulsions and bloodshed to a military despotism. Instead of universal suffrage therefore, I would have one of the two County Members, or an additonal County Member if that should be preferred in every shire, represented *exclusively* by this description of people, in the following manner: Let the labourers of every parish in each county, and they can easily be distinguished by their own parish officers ; let the labourers of each parish choose one elector out of their own number, to nominate the member that is to represent them, and let it be established by law, that these members must possess *bona-fide* property, in the county which they represent, to the amount of £600 per annum. Instead of the insignificant title of Knights of the shire, those members might be styled advocates of the people; and, as it would be their business to acquire a thorough knowledge of the real condition of the poor in their respective counties,

---

* If it should be argued that universal suffrage was not adopted at the time of the Parliamentary war, I reply that, at that time, the efforts of the Parliament, without the voluntary aid of the peop , would have been too feeble to produce any effect serious consequence; and this amounts to the same thing as universal suffrage,

and their interest to endeavour to acquire an influence over them by acts of kindness and benevolence, they would necessarily become a sort of mediators between the rich and the poor, the labourers and their employers. These admonitions and good advice would prevent oppression on the one hand and turbulence on the other; and, without the possibility of endangering the constitution, they would, in this way, be really beneficial; for, so long as they maintained only the just rights of the people, their united remonstrances, backed by the voice of the people out of doors, would be sure to procure immediate redress; while their numbers would be too few to carry any measure that was really injurious to the state.

FINIS.

HISTORICAL SKETCH

OF THE

K OF ENGLAND:

WITH AN

ιMINATION OF THE QUESTION

AS TO THE PROLONGATION OF

EXCLUSIVE PRIVILEGES

OF

THAT - ESTABLISHMENT.

LONDON:

PRINTED FOR

GMAN, REES, ORME, BROWN, & GREEN,

PATERNOSTER ROW.

1831.

7.—1725, 12th George I. c. 34.—If any clothier, &c. &c. or any person concerned in employing workmen in the woollen manufacture, shall pay their wages, either in *goods*, or by way of *truck*, or in any other manner, than in money, contrary to the true intent and meaning of this act, the offender to pay a penalty of £10.

8.—1726, 13th George I. c. 23.—The foregoing clause re-enacted, and extended to the manufacture of leather, with the additional provision of (except and at their request and by their consent only).

9.—1736, 9th George II. c. 23.—Restricts the payment of workmen in spirituous liquors, as part of their wages.

10.—1749, 22d George II. c. 27.—The former prohibitions against paying wages either in *goods*, or *by way of truck*, or in *any other manner than money*, re-enacted; and extended to the manufacture of hats, silk, mohair, fur, hemp, flax, linen, cotton, fustian, iron, or leather, or any mixt materials. Penalty £10.

11.—1756, 29th George II. c. 33.—For the regulation and better payment of the wages of persons employed in the woollen manufactures, prohibits payment either in *goods*, *truck*, *bill*, or *note*, or in any other manner, than in money, augmenting the penalty to £20.

12.—1757, 30th George II. c. 12.—Permits work in the woollen manufactory to be done by contract; but restricts the payment of the wages to money, and to be paid two days after the delivery of the work, under a penalty of 40s.

13.—1779, 19th George III. c. 49.—Enacts that all persons who shall employ any manufacturers of thread lace, or who shall purchase lace of them, shall pay them in money only, and not with goods, notwithstanding any usage or custom to the contrary, under a penalty of £10.

14.—1817, 57th George III. c. 115.—Prohibits the payment of wages in goods, or by way of truck, or otherwise than in the lawful coin of this realm, to workmen employed in articles made of steel, plated articles, and cutlery. Penalty £10.

15.—1817, 57th George III. c. 122.—The same provisions extended to labourers in collieries.

1'.—1818, 58th George III. c. 151.—The whole of the provisions of the fore-going acts consolidated, with permission to masters to pay such workmen, *as shall be willing to receive the same*, in Bank of England or Country Bankers' Notes.

17.—1820.—1st George IV. c. 98.—Prohibits masters from making any stipulation or agreement either directly or indirectly, as to the place or manner of laying out the wages paid to their workmen. Penalty £10 to £20.

18.—1775, 15th George III. c. 00.—Preamble of the Act for restraining the negociation of *Promissory Notes under 20s.*—"Whereas various Notes, Bills of Exchange, and Drafts for Money, for very small sums, have for some time past been circulated or negociated in lieu of cash within that part of Great Britain called England, to the great prejudice of trade and p bli credit; and many such bills and drafts being payable under certain terms and restrictions, which the poorer sort of manufacturers, artificers, labourers, and others, cannot comply with, otherwise than by being subject to *great extortion and abuse*."

18.—1777, 17th George III. c. 30.—Part of the Preamble to the Act for further restraining the negociation of Promissory Notes under the amount of £5.—"And whereas the said act (see above) hath been attended with very salutary effects, and in case the provisions therein contained were extended to a further sum, the good purpose of the said act would be further advanced," &c. &c."

HERNAMAN AND PERRING, PRINTERS, 20, COMMERCIAL-STREET, LEEDS.

CPSIA information can be obtained
at www.ICGtesting.com
Printed in the USA
BVHW040250231118
533509BV00032BB/4731/P

9 781334 472589